1000
Things to
Draw

Designed and illustrated by
Carly Davies

Written by Kirsteen Robson

In this book there are lots of suggestions
of things to draw. The circled numbers
on the pages tell you how many things
to draw to add up exactly to 1000.

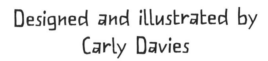

Choose 5 flowers to copy in the spaces, then draw 5 bees and 4 butterflies.

Draw another jellyfish like each of these and add 10 bubbles of different sizes.

9

Copy each shell shape twice,
then draw 3 pieces of seaweed.

Copy each of these 5 boats once. Then, draw 10 birds flying around them.

Draw 4 copies of this snail and
give each one a swirly trail.

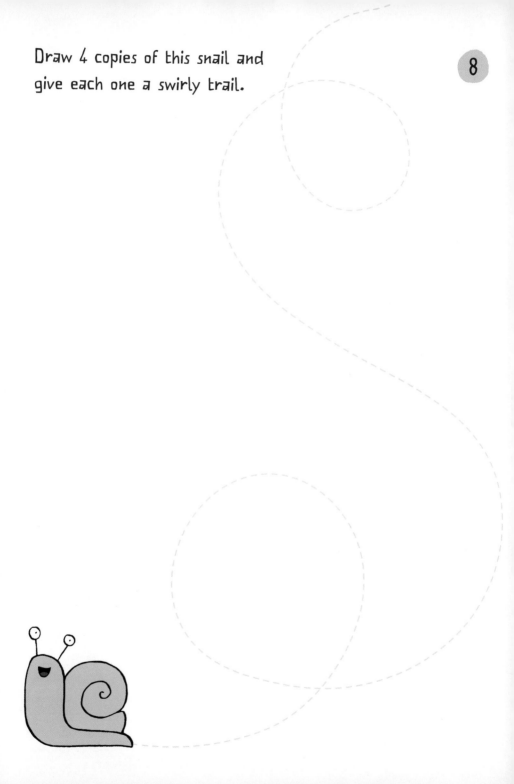

Sketch 2 more stalks and draw 3 leaves on each one. Then, choose 9 of these bugs to copy.

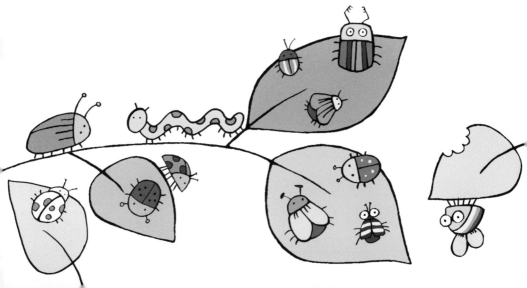

Use these ideas to design 6 buildings of your own. Finish your picture by adding 4 more trees.

Copy each of these delivery vans once and give all 6 vans a driver.

Draw 4 more cups or cones, each filled with ice cream. Finish them with 2 chocolate flakes and 2 wafers.

Copy each fish shape and decorate it as you like. Now draw 3 clumps of water weeds, too.

Draw 6 more socks hanging on the line, then copy the other 3 items once.

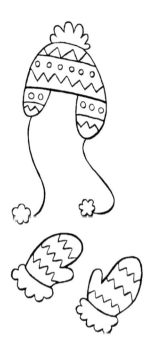

18

Draw and decorate 6 hats and
12 mittens, in matching pairs.

Use the ideas below to draw 6 more desserts. Top them with 2 strawberries, 2 cherries, a leaf and a little umbrella.

Here are some hot snacks. Add to
them by drawing 3 hot dogs, 4 burgers
and 5 pizzas of your own design.

Draw a twin for each alien.
Then, add 4 more shooting stars.

Copy 3 of the containers twice and fill them with bubbling liquids. Add 4 stirring sticks and 3 puffs of steam.

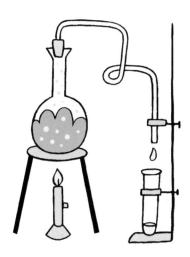

Draw a copy of each horse.
Give each animal a blanket,
then draw 5 tufts of grass.

Copy each bucket once and draw
3 sand castles to match them. Give each
castle a flag and 2 pebble windows.

Cover 10 party flags with doodly patterns,
then add fancy edges to 8 of them.

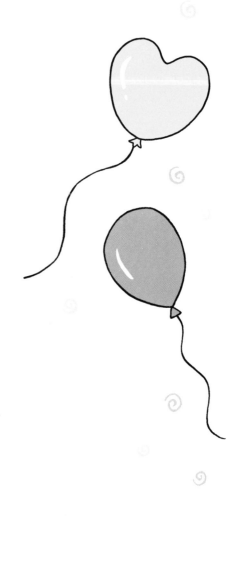

Draw and decorate 5 more balloons.

Draw each snake shape twice,
then decorate them differently.

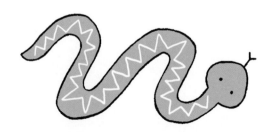

Draw 4 patterned pots like these and
put a prickly cactus plant in each one.

Use the ideas below to draw 6 cupcakes.

Copy each jar shape once, then design a
jar of your own. Fill all 5 jars with goodies.

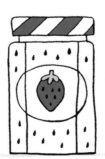
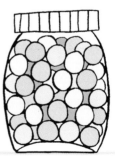

Draw 2 copies of each gift
box shape. Draw a label
and a ribbon on each one.

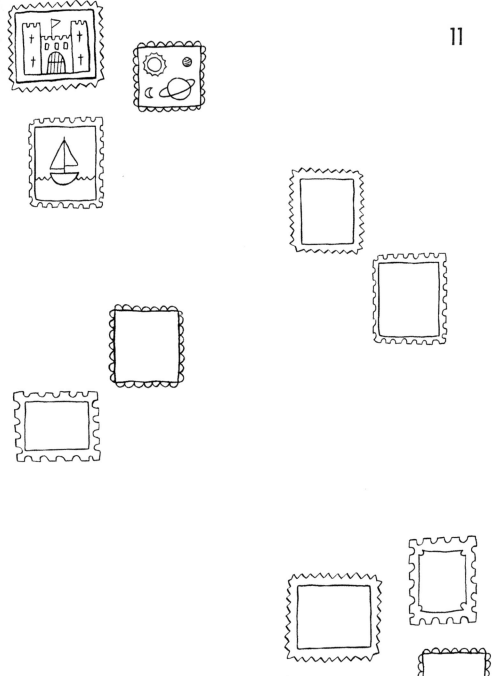

Draw a different picture on each of these
7 stamps, then draw 4 stamps of your own.

Draw 2 leaves, 3 caterpillars,
4 dragonflies, 5 moths and 6 spiders.

Copy each spaceship once and draw an alien in each one to fly it. Then, draw 7 more stars.

Draw 3 more monsters waiting to greet the aliens. You can copy these or make up monsters of your own.

Draw a copy of each watch and
then design a watch of your own.

Copy or design 8 more keys.

Here are 2 elephants. Copy them both once, then draw a plant.

Draw 2 giraffes just like these,
then copy the leafy branch.

Copy each car twice and give
each car a driver. Then, draw
a dog in 3 of the cars.

Draw 14 leaves of
various shapes and sizes.

Copy the fox and squirrel once, then
draw 2 hedgehogs and 5 flowers.

Copy each perching bird onto an empty twig
and draw 3 birds flying around them.

Draw and decorate 5 umbrellas.
Now draw 4 clouds, bringing
4 kinds of weather.

Choose 2 crocodiles to copy,
and draw another bird.

Copy each of these 5 vegetables twice.

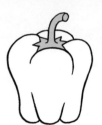

Draw a watering can,
3 packets of seeds, 2 little
plant pots, a fork and a trowel.

Draw a copy of each robot, then design 2 robots of your own.

Copy each dinosaur, then draw 5 plants.

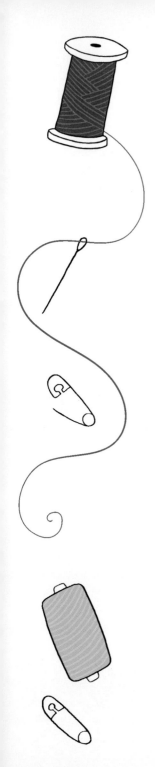

14

Copy each of these 3 spools once and
draw a thread trailing from each one.
Then, draw 4 needles and 4 safety-pins.

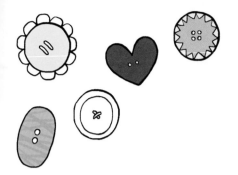

Draw 6 round, 5 square,
4 star-shaped, 3 flower-shaped
and 2 heart-shaped buttons.

Draw 3 sheep just like these. Then, draw 4 flowers and 2 tufts of grass.

Copy each pig twice,
then draw 2 buckets.

6

Draw and decorate 3 pairs of boots.
Then, draw 2 puddles and 6 raindrops.

Copy or design 6 hats and draw
a hatstand under 2 of them.

Choose 2 cows to copy.
Then, add 2 tufts of
grass and 2 flowers.

Copy each of these chickens once. Now
draw a nest and put 3 eggs inside it.

Use these ideas to copy or design 3 pots. Give each one a swirl of steam.

Draw and decorate
6 cups or mugs.

Copy each dog once and draw
1 more shelter. Then, draw
4 bowls and 4 bones.

Draw 4 tents and 3 trees.

Copy each toadstool shape once,
then decorate them as you like.
Draw a tiny bug on 2 of them.

Choose 2 windmills to copy,
or draw 2 of your own design.

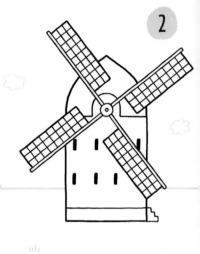

Here are 3 hot-air balloons. Copy each
balloon once, then draw 3 clouds.

There are 5 penguins here. Copy each one once, giving 2 of them hats and 2 of them scarves.

Draw 4 picture frames, then
fill the 6 empty frames with
a different picture.

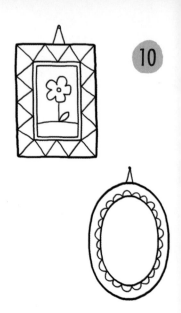

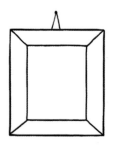

Here are 6 chicks. Copy each
chick once, then draw 2 eggs
just starting to hatch.

Copy each lion twice to draw 4 more.

Choose 3 kittens to copy. Then, draw 3 mouse
toys and a ball of yarn for them to play with.

Copy each rocket shape once. Now
fill the spaces between them with
3 planets, 2 space rocks and 6 stars.

Draw 3 kites with long tails,
and 2 birds flying nearby.

Copy each plane shape once.
Now draw 4 clouds around them.

Copy each crab twice, then draw 1 starfish, 2 strands of seaweed and 3 pebbles.

Draw 4 frozen treats. Copy
these or create your own.

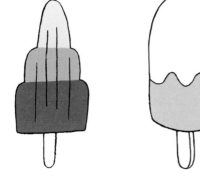   

Copy each bunny once.
Now, draw 4 flowers.

Draw 6 egg shapes and fill each
one with a different pattern.

Copy each of the 4 big starfish
twice, then draw 3 smaller starfish.

Draw 2 copies of each bag shape, then
decorate all 8 bags any way you like.

Choose a monkey in a palm tree to copy. Now copy the dangling monkey twice and give both of them a bunch of bananas.

Copy each bird cage once. Now draw a bird
inside each cage and 2 more that have escaped.

Draw 10 more pea pods. Give each
one a leaf and a twisting tendril.

Draw 3 swirly lollipops
and 4 fizzy snakes.
Then, copy 7 other sugary
treats around them.

Draw 5 busy bees and give
each one a buzzy trail.

Copy each duck twice,
then draw 2 plants on
the riverbank.

There are 11 trees here.
Copy each tree once. Now
draw 3 birds and 2 owls.

16

Use these ideas to draw 5 cakes or slices. Give
one of them 3 candles or 3 stars on sticks.

Copy each fruit once, then draw 5 others, such as oranges, pears or grapes.

Sketch 4 stalks and give each one a different flower. Now copy each butterfly shape and decorate the wings as you like.

Draw 4 octopus babies –
just like these, but smaller.

Copy each turtle once. Now draw 2 more, with different patterns on their shells.

Here are 3 big machines. Copy
each machine once, then draw
3 workers to operate them.

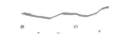

Draw 3 snowmen and give
each one a hat and a scarf.
Now draw 10 snowflakes
swirling around them.

Use these ideas to design 12
dangling decorations of your own.

Choose 3 birdhouses to copy
and draw 3 little birds nearby.

Copy each vase shape once and decorate them any way you like. Then, draw 9 flowers.

Sketch 22 stems and use
the ideas below to draw
a variety of plants.

There are 4 pets here.
Copy each animal once and
draw 3 more bowls of food.

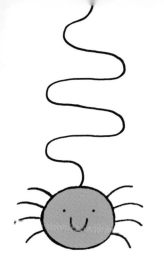

Draw 4 spiders and 4 flies.

Draw 8 socks and decorate them.

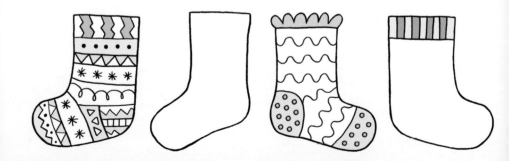

Copy each surfboard shape once, then
draw patterns on the 4 blank boards.

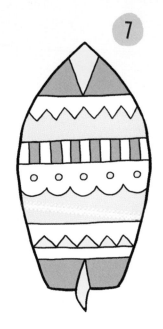

Copy each chameleon twice. Then,
add 4 leaves to the picture.

8

Here are 3 geckos. Copy
them to draw 3 more.

Choose 7 butterfly shapes to copy
and decorate. Then, draw 7 flowers.

Copy each of these 3 mermaids
and add 7 bubbles.

Use these ideas to draw 4 crowns or tiaras. Then, draw 7 gems.

Draw a nest with chicks inside it. Then,
copy each of the 3 perching birds twice.

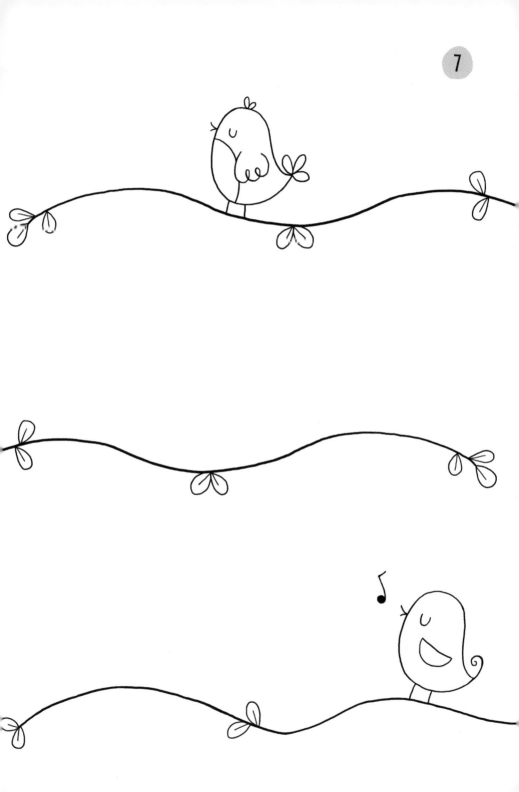

Copy each bat once.
Now draw 7 stars.

Draw 4 ghosts and give each
face a different expression.

Here is a lily pond. Copy each frog once,
then draw 3 lily leaves and 3 flowers.

Copy these owl shapes to show 2 owls standing
on branches and 2 that have just jumped off.